Wedding Favours

Wedding Favours

Antonia Swinson

RYLAND
PETERS
& SMALL

LONDON NEW YORK

Senior Designer Sonya Nathoo
Editor Martha Keenan
Commissioning Editor Annabel Morgan
Picture Researcher Emily Westlake
Production Gemma Moules
Art Director Anne-Marie Bulat
Editorial Director Julia Charles
Publishing Director Alison Starling

First published in Great Britain
in 2006 by Ryland Peters & Small
20–21 Jockey's Fields
London WC1R 4BW
www.rylandpeters.com

10 9 8 7 6 5 4 3 2 1
Text, design and photographs
© Ryland Peters & Small 2006

ISBN-10: 1 84597 105 1
ISBN-13: 978 1 84597 105 2

A CIP record for this book is available from
the British Library.

Printed in China

contents

introduction

Everyone loves being given a present. Handing out mementoes, or favours, to wedding guests is a time-honoured tradition, a small but significant way in which the bride and groom can say thank you to friends and family for their generosity, support and good wishes.

As with any gift, the thought is more important than the contents, and for those on a budget, there are dozens of ideas here for favours that are every bit as cost-effective as they are appealing. There are delicious edible goodies, such as biscuits, cakes, chocolates and sweets (many of which can be made at home), as well as flowers, candles and scented gifts; and luxurious keepsakes for special members of the wedding party. There are also ideas galore for beautiful packaging and fabulous presentation.

Whatever your taste, creative abilities and budget, you're sure to find something that both you and your guests will love!

fabulous favours

What will you delight your wedding guests with? Whatever your taste and budget, there are favours to suit: delectable cakes, biscuits, chocolates and sweets; dainty napkins and handkerchiefs; romantic flowers; scented delights; magical candles; beautiful bags; and special keepsakes.

edible goodies

BISCUITS

Biscuits are an inexpensive but universally popular choice of favour. Whether home-made or shop bought, there is a choice of biscuits that are buttery and plain, macaroon-crumbly, perfumed with vanilla or lemon, or studded with chocolate chips or nuts. For an autumn or winter wedding, biscuits laced with sweet spices such as cinnamon, ginger or cloves – or, more extravagantly, gleaming with real gold leaf – would evoke the season perfectly.

Shaped biscuits always look appealing. Cutters can be bought in every conceivable shape and size from specialist shops and mail-order suppliers. Hearts are an obvious and undeniably romantic choice, or you could opt for stars, flowers, butterflies, birds or your initials. If you want to decorate your biscuits, try colour co-ordinating them with the flowers or wedding dress for a professional look. A simple, smooth coating of royal icing looks

Distributing favours to friends and family is a symbolic gesture with ancient roots, a recognition of the guests' role in supporting and witnessing the marriage.

effective and can be further embellished with gold or silver balls, sugar flowers or sparkling coloured sugars and powders, which are available from cake-decorating suppliers.

If you're an experienced home cook or are having your biscuits professionally made, they could be iced with intricate patterns or a motif that has a special meaning for you. They could even be shaped and decorated to look like miniature wedding cakes. Biscuits could also be iced with initials or names, whether yours or those of your guests. If biscuits are iced with guests' names, they can double up as place markers, as shown on page 13. Here, rectangular biscuits imitate name tags, iced in delicious pastel shades and finished with matching ribbon (just remember to pierce the hole before baking).

Fine ribbon can also be used to hang biscuits up for display, perhaps from branches held in a vase or, in winter, from Christmas trees and ivy wreaths. Biscuits also look good packaged in boxes (see opposite, above right), nestling in paper-lined punnets (below left), or laid out on a platter of rose petals.

CUPCAKES

During a ceremony called *confarreatio,* the most binding form of marriage in ancient Rome, the bridal couple shared a sweet cake. Presenting your guests with cake favours echoes this and many other centuries-old wedding traditions. Like biscuits, cakes can easily be produced at home and are a versatile vehicle for decoration.

Cupcakes have simple charm and can be topped with icing and other goodies, such as chocolate curls, sugar flowers, gold or silver balls, crystallized fresh flowers, sweets, fresh fruit or gold leaf. They can also be

iced with names or initials. Even simple shop-bought cakes, such as the pastel-coloured ones shown on the left, look tempting when presented with flair.

Another approach is to give each guest a miniature wedding cake, iced to resemble its full-scale parent. For a December wedding, tiny Christmas cakes might be fun. Other sweet mouthfuls to consider include tiny scones and miniature tarts or chocolate torte.

CHOCOLATES

When it comes to luxury, few things beat luscious, indulgent chocolate. Prettily packaged (here, in a box printed with antique engravings, lined with tissue and tied with ribbon), they'll be irresistible to your guests.

If your budget allows, you could splash out on handmade chocolates such as palest pink white-chocolate truffles (see page 21), sumptuous continental-style chocolates or old-fashioned rose or violet creams. A professional chocolatier may be able to personalize your chocolates with a motif, name or initials, using dark chocolate against white, or vice versa, for a striking contrast.

If money's more of an issue, chocolate truffles are easy to produce at home from chocolate, cream and various flavourings (such as vanilla or liqueur), and your guests will undoubtedly appreciate the effort you've put into them. If you're making your own, it's worth using really good-quality chocolate with a 70 per cent cocoa solids content. Home-made truffles can be rolled in cocoa powder or chopped nuts (try almonds or pistachios), or dipped in melted chocolate (see page 20).

Wrapped chocolates are another option. Here (left), golden hearts have been placed in a wineglass to double up as place markers, complete with co-ordinating gold name tags. For variations on the chocolate theme, consider chocolate-covered coffee beans to be brought round with coffee, chocolate-dipped miniature meringues or chocolate-dipped fruit. For a spring wedding, offer chocolate eggs in little baskets lined with moss and primroses.

Chocolates of all kinds look elegant in petit four cases, tucked inside paper cones or placed in cellophane bags tied with fancy ribbon. If you're going to bring them out at the end of the meal, you could wrap them in twists of brightly coloured tissue paper and pile them into coffee cups (see page 58).

SWEETS

For favours with a bit of fun and frivolity, sweets are a great choice. Sugared almonds are one of the most popular favours, and have a long association with weddings (the Romans threw sweet almonds over newlyweds, a practice which developed into throwing confetti). Almonds have for centuries been associated with fertility and abundance, and it's traditional to give guests five to represent health, wealth, happiness, fertility and long life. Sugared almonds are a versatile choice, too, because they're available in a huge range of colours to co-ordinate with any scheme. They look wonderful piled into dishes such as the one shown on the left, which doubles as a table number, or tied up in small circles of paper or fabric.

Jelly beans also come in lots of tempting colours and flavours, though for a more sophisticated approach you might like to stick to

just one (above, white beans look elegant in cellophane cones finished with mint-green ribbon). Just as chic are the white mints shown here in cellophane bundles. Pastel dolly mixtures, jelly babies, sticks of rock, candy love hearts or fruity lollipops will no doubt encourage your guests to revisit their childhoods and should provoke a smile or two. Present sweets in bags or boxes, or fill baskets with them and invite your guests to pick and mix. You could even sprinkle your tables with edible confetti.